Food Groups

Fruits

Lola Schaefer

Heinemann
LIBRARY

www.heinemann.co.uk/library
Visit our website to find out more information about Heinemann Library books.

To order:
☎ Phone 44 (0) 1865 888066
▤ Send a fax to 44 (0) 1865 314091
▢ Visit the Heinemann Bookshop at www.heinemann.co.uk/library to browse our catalogue and order online.

First published in Great Britain by Heinemann Library, Halley Court, Jordan Hill, Oxford OX2 8EJ, part of Pearson Education. Heinemann is a registered trademark of Pearson Education Ltd.

© Pearson Education Ltd 2008
First published in paperback in 2008
The moral right of the proprietor has been asserted.

Editorial: Diyan Leake and Kristen Truhlar
Design: Joanna Hinton-Malivoire
Picture research: Melissa Allison
Artwork: Big Top
Production: Duncan Gilbert
Originated by Modern Age
Printed and bound in China by South China Printing Co. Ltd

ISBN 978 0 431 01519 4 (hardback)
12 11 10 09 08
10 9 8 7 6 5 4 3 2

ISBN 978 0 431 01526 2 (paperback)
12 11 10 09 08
10 9 8 7 6 5 4 3 2 1

British Library Cataloguing in Publication Data
Schaefer, Lola M., 1950-
Fruit. - (Food groups)
1. Fruit - Juvenile literature 2. Fruit in human nutrition - Juvenile literature 3. Cookery (Fruit) - Juvenile literature
I. Title
641.3'4

Acknowledgements
The publishers would like to thank the following for permission to reproduce photographs: © Digital Vision p. **29**; © Getty Images pp. **14** (Taxi), **20** (Photonica/Jonathan Knowles), **26** (Food Collection), **28** (Dorling Kindersley); © Harcourt Education Ltd pp. **4** (Tudor Photography), **9** (MM Studios), **11** (Tudor Photography), **12** (Tudor Photography), **16** (Tudor Photography), **19** (Tudor Photography), **21** (MM Studios), **24** (Tudor Photography), **25** (Tudor Photography); © KPT Power Photos pp. **10** (banana, blueberry, kiwi, peach), **21**; © Photodisc pp. **10** (apple), **18**; © Photolibrary.com pp. **6** (Picture Press), **7** (Jtb Photocommunications Inc.), **13** (Foodpix); © Photolibrary pp. **22** (Anthony Blake), **27** (David M. Dennis); © Punchstock pp. **15** (Comstock), **17** (BananaStock), **23** (Creatas).

Cover photograph reproduced with permission © Masterfile (Michael Mahovlich).

Every effort has been made to contact copyright holders of any material reproduced in this book. Any omissions will be rectified in subsequent printings if notice is given to the publishers.

Contents

Some words are shown in bold, **like this**. You can find out what they mean by looking in the glossary.

What are fruits?

Fruits are the sweet food that grows on some plants. Plums, strawberries, apples, and grapes are all fruits. People all over the world eat fruits every day.

Fruits have natural sugars in them that make them taste sweet.

Each colour on this plate is for one of the five food groups.

Fruits are one of the **food groups**. You need to eat fruits each day as part of a good **diet**. Fresh fruits help your body fight illness and keep you healthy.

Where fruits come from

Fruits grow on flowering plants. Cherries grow on trees in **orchards**. Grapes grow on vines on **arbors**. Raspberries grow on bushes in rows on farms. Melons grow on vines in fields.

Bananas only grow in warm places, but they are shipped all over the world.

Strawberries are grown outside both in the ground and in pots.

Some people grow their own fruits in their gardens. They have berry bushes or fruit trees. These people enjoy eating the fresh fruit that they grow.

Using fruits

Most fruits are picked and then eaten just as they are. Sometimes fruits are squeezed and made into juice. Apple and orange juice are healthy drinks. Many juices are a mix of different fruits.

Try to find fruit juices with no added sugar. These are the healthiest juices.

sultanas

cranberries

raisins

apricots

banana

Dried fruit is full of **fibre**.

Many fruits are dried. The water is taken from the fruit and the fruit becomes smaller and chewy. Raisins are dried grapes. Prunes are dried plums.

What fruits look like

Fruits can be small like berries or grapes. They may be large like pineapples or watermelons. Many fruits have a round shape, but some fruits are long like bananas.

Fruits come in different colours and sizes.

Fruits can be green, red, yellow, orange, blue, white, pink, or purple. Many berries have bumpy outsides. Blueberries are dark blue and have smooth outsides.

How fruits taste

Almost all fruits taste sweet. That is why people like to eat fruit. Some fruits can have a **sour** taste. A lemon or lime tastes sour.

Lemon juice helps sliced fruits stay bright and fresh.

Many people like to slice avocado on top of their salads.

Some fruits, like avocados, have a different taste. The inside of an avocado tastes a little oily. Avocados can be eaten by themselves, in salads, or in sandwiches.

Why fruits are healthy

Fruits are healthy because they have less **fat** than other foods. They also have many **vitamins**, **minerals**, and **fibre**. These are important **nutrients** that the body uses.

Fruits also contain juice, which has water. Water helps keep the body healthy.

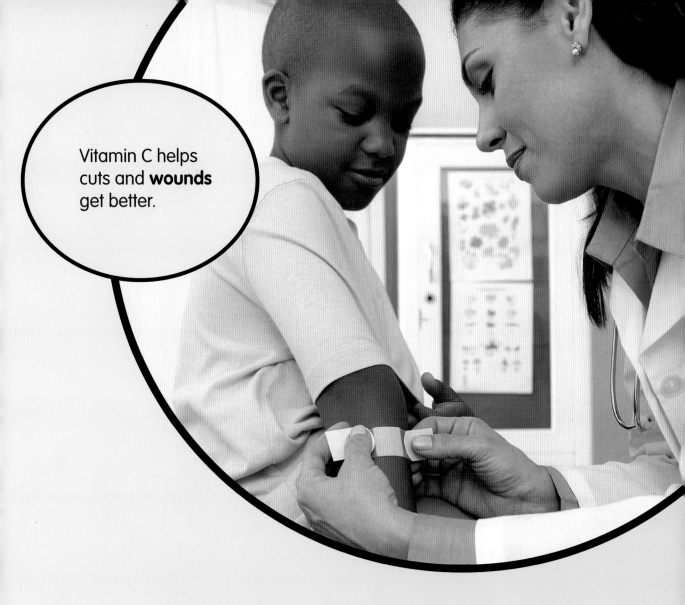

Vitamin C helps cuts and **wounds** get better.

The vitamins and minerals in fruits help keep you healthy. Many fresh fruits have vitamin C. It helps fight colds and other illnesses.

How many fruits do you need?

Most children 5–10 years old need 1–2 servings of fruits each day. You could eat one pear for one of your servings. Or you could eat a slice of melon.

There are many different fruits to choose your servings from.

Eat a few different fruits every day to stay healthy.

A small handful of dried fruit is the same as a serving of fresh fruit. Try a handful of raisins or apricots. One glass of fruit juice is also a serving.

Fruits to eat for breakfast

Many people start the morning with a glass of orange, grapefruit, or apple juice. Other people enjoy a bowl of fresh fruit with their toast or muffin. Some eat sliced fruit on cereal.

Fruit salad is a healthy and tasty treat for breakfast.

Try to find jam with little or no added sugar. These are the healthiest jams for your body.

You can add fresh fruit to many breakfast foods. Some people add blueberries to pancakes. Others eat fruit salad with yoghurt poured on top. Fruit jam on toast adds flavour.

Fruits to eat for lunch

Many people eat fruit at the end of their lunch. People sometimes eat an apple, a sliced kiwi, or a banana. People also have a glass of juice.

The skin of fruit helps protect it while it travels from one place to another.

Fruit kebabs

Please ask an adult to help you.

- Wash or peel the fruit.
- Have an adult cut the fruit into bite-sized pieces.
- Squirt each piece with lemon juice.
- Place the cut fruit on large toothpicks or kebab sticks.
- Serve and enjoy. You could try these dipped in your favorite yoghurt.

You will need:
- three fruits from this list: strawberries, watermelon pieces, seedless grapes, apple slices, pears, bananas, peaches
- large toothpicks or kebab sticks
- lemon juice

Fruits to eat for dinner

For dinner, you can add fruit to salads, rice, or noodles. Some people like pears and cheese or peaches with cottage cheese. But most people eat fresh fruit at the end of their dinner.

For a dinner treat, ask your parent to slice a star fruit to see how this fruit got its name.

Fruits are often served as part of a dinner with meat.

Sometimes fruits are used in sauces for meat. Apple sauce can be served with roast pork. Cranberry sauce is normally eaten with roast turkey.

Fruits to eat for snacks

Fresh fruit is a great healthy snack. Many people drink a glass of fruit juice for quick **energy**. Dried fruit is a good snack to eat.

Raisins are made when the water is dried from grapes.

Fruit juice-icles

Please ask an adult to help you.

- Pour fruit juice into the cups and fill ¾ of the way.
- Place in the freezer.
- Put a lolly stick in the juice when it is almost frozen.
- Put the cups back into the freezer until the juice is frozen solid.
- Remove the juice-icle from the cup.
- Serve and enjoy.

You will need:
- 8 small paper or plastic cups
- 8 lolly sticks
- your favourite fruit juice (without added sugar)

Juice-icles are a great treat on a warm day.

Keeping fruits fresh

Ripe fruit needs to be stored in a cool place. Some fruits such as strawberries, raspberries, and blueberries keep best in the refrigerator. Bananas are one fruit that should not be put in the refrigerator. It spoils the taste.

Apples, oranges, and pears can be kept in a fruit bowl in a cool room.

Do not eat fruits that have mould.

Be careful. If you see **mould** on the outside of fruit, do not eat it. It is not good for your body. It is best to eat fruit soon after you have bought it.

Do fruits alone keep you healthy?

Fruits are good foods for your body. But you need many different foods to stay healthy. Eat from each **food group** every day and drink three or four glasses of water.

By eating different foods, you will get all the **nutrients** that your body needs.

Exercise every day and keep your muscles strong.

As well as eating healthy foods, your body needs regular **exercise**. You should try to get a little each day. You also need to get plenty of sleep each night. Sleep helps you stay strong and well.

Glossary

arbor garden support or fence that holds grape vines

diet what a person usually eats and drinks

energy power needed for a body to work and stay alive

exercise physical activity that helps keep a body healthy and fit

fat nutrient in food that gives the body energy. The body only needs a little fat each day.

fibre rough part of food that is not digested. Fibre helps carry food through the body.

food group foods that have the same kind of nutrients. There are five main food groups, plus oils.

mineral nutrient needed to make the body work correctly

mould furry fungus that grows on old or spoiled food

nutrient substance (such as a vitamin or mineral) that the body needs to stay healthy and grow

orchard piece of land used to grow fruit or nut trees

sour sharp taste

vitamin nutrient in food that the body needs to stay healthy. Nutrients help the body work correctly.

wound where the skin is torn, broken, or cut

Find out more

Books to read

Go Facts: Healthy Eating, Paul McEvoy (A & C Black, 2005)

Look After Yourself: Eat Healthy Food!, Angela Royston (Heinemann Library, 2004)

What's on Your Plate? Breakfast, Ted and Lola Schaefer (Raintree, 2006)

Websites to visit

www.5aday.nhs.uk
Click on "Fun & Games" and then "Did You Know?" to find out amazing fruit facts.

www.childrenfirst.nhs.uk/kids/health/eat_smart/food_science/index.html
Click on the fruits on the tray to find out more about why these are good for you and how many you need to eat each day.

www.nutrition.org.uk
Click on "Cook Club" for some great recipe ideas.

Index